Straight with the Medicine

Straight with the Medicine

NARRATIVES OF WASHOE FOLLOWERS
OF THE TIPI WAY
AS TOLD TO

Warren L. d'Azevedo

HEYDAY BOOKS, BERKELEY

Straight with the Medicine was originally printed in 1978 in an edition of 105 copies on an 1837 super-royal Columbian handpress at the University of Nevada, Reno, Library by Kenneth J. Carpenter of the Black Rock Press. The type faces were Centaur and Arrighi, hand set. The paper was Tovil, an English handmade, and printed damp. The inks were Mandlik and Kelsey.

The woodcuts were rendered on plywood by the printer and the designs were either his own emblematic illustration for a particular narrative or were derived from a traditional symbol associated with the Peyote Way.

The present edition is, except for details in the front and back matter, a photo offset reproduction of the original, reduced to 75% of the original size.

Cover design by Sarah Levin

Published by
Heyday Books
P.O. Box 9145
Berkeley, California 94709

ISBN: 0-930588-19-3

10 9 8 7 6 5 4 3 2 1

Contents

TO PAUL RADIN, GEORGE LEITE
AND THOSE SEVEN MEN OF THE
WASHOE NATION WHO SPOKE THE
WORDS THAT HAVE BEEN MADE
INTO THIS BOOK

Preface

The men whose words have been made into this book were members of the Washoe Tribe living in the valleys of western Nevada and on the eastern slopes of the Sierra in California. They were followers of the Native American Church, a small group within the tribe whose sacrament was the Peyote cactus and who referred to their religion as the Tipi Way.

When I first met these men in the early 1950's, the Peyote religion had been among the Washoe people for scarcely more than fifteen years. Though many tribes of North America have known it for at least a century, it did not appear in western Nevada until Sam Lone Bear held meetings among the Northern Paiute in the late 1920's. In 1936 a Washoe man, Ben Lancaster, returned to the area after a long sojourn abroad and announced that he had come to bring the new religion to his people. Together with his friend, Sam Dick, a former shaman, he held meetings in the scattered Indian settlements, attracting many Washoe and Paiute adherents. It was not long, however, before a deep reaction set in against the movement, led by a few outraged traditional shamans and some white ministers and medical practitioners who saw it as a threat to their domains. Many ceased to participate, and the remaining believers were forced to meet in secret places remote from white towns and hostile neighbors. For a time, the movement became defensive and factionalism appeared among the Peyotists themselves. Yet they were united in looking upon their religion as the only answer to the desperate poverty, alcoholism and apathy which was destroying the lives of so many of their people. Thus, the most compelling themes of these narratives are of a search for a more meaningful life, for personal dignity, and the rediscovery of the positive values of an Indian past which had been dimmed by a century of conquest and degradation. The goal is expressed not as individual salvation or personal quest for power, but always as a collective endeavour, a helping of one another and a unity with nature.

In the process of writing down the words these men have spoken, and preparing them for presentation, I have devoted every effort of which I am capable to record accurately and meaningfully what I heard. As an outsider, it would be presumptuous of me to believe that I could grasp the whole of the reality they were experiencing, or venture to speak for them. They were my friends who did their utmost to instruct me about their beliefs and innermost thoughts. I feel it an obligation to let them speak for themselves. Certain of the narratives were transcribed directly from tape recordings made during sessions of prayer and singing when the participants had overcome the deep reluctance which, in those days, some felt about the use of such devices. However, most of the narratives were taken from my notes written during informal discussions, and they have been selected, abridged or rearranged for presentation here. They were told under a variety of circumstances and represent different intents on the part of the speakers. Some are accounts of personal experiences or preachment in response to my efforts to understand what I saw and heard. Others are versions of well-known tales exchanged by Peyotists throughout the country and told for both entertainment and moral instruction. The individual speakers are not identified and I have attempted to remove any direct references to living persons or to specific localities that might reveal identities and violate confidences,

I have tried to retain the quality of the speech without recourse to grammatical revision or any of the conventional devices for altering the written form of English words to indicate how they might actually be pronounced. Except for capitalization of certain terms having a sacred or unique traditional value, much has been left to the reader's eye and ear; for my purpose has been to conserve as fully as possible the eloquent rhythm and intonation of the spoken language without artificial aids. The Washoe speak their own language slowly and with a quiet dignity, particularly in public discourse. There are long thoughtful pauses while each phrase is pondered for meaning and effect, or repeated until the cadence of speech is merged with mood and content. Many of these narratives retain the recitative quality appropriate to earnest matters. The reader will also become aware of the subtle and sometimes sharp edge of humor which is an irrepressible element in Washoe culture, often taking

the form of unexpected satirical thrusts at the pompous and incongru-
ous, just as the use of exaggerated self-effacement may be employed to
deflate conceit or rivalry. Yet always central to the narratives is the sol-
emn and rigorous dedication to the Peyote Way, to the emancipation
of one's self and one's fellows from ignominy and helplessness. The
message is one of new-found hope and the discovery of purpose.

The Washoe people have made great advances since the 1950's. They
have succeeded in winning compensation for white encroachment on
ancient lands and, through effective use of funds from new government
programs, have made rapid improvements in housing, education, em-
ployment and tribal organization. The wretched conditions of the recent
past seem all but obliterated, and many young people are scarcely aware
of the quite different world in which their parents and grandparents clung
to a precarious existence. Today the tribe, numbering about two thou-
sand people, proudly refers to itself as the Washoe Nation. Young people
have begun to take a lively interest in tribal affairs, and many of them
hold important professional and leadership positions in the larger community. It is for these young persons, as well as for their older relatives,
that the words spoken by some of their own people in the decade of the
1950's may have the most meaning. Though some of the issues and forms
of expression may now seem outmoded, there is an enduring reality that
will awaken a profound sense of identity. The Peyotist religion has per-
sisted among a small group of the Washoe people to this day, but its
followers are now part of the mainstream of local community life. The
antagonisms that once characterized tribal relations have given way to a
tolerance of the religion as one of the many manifestations of the Native
American struggle for regeneration of the values and self-esteem of a
vigorous heritage.

The encouragement and guidance of many persons contributed to the
work of which these narratives are but a part. To each of them I owe the
fullest extent of gratitude. I want to add a special note of appreciation
to Kenneth Carpenter for his keen respect for these narratives and his
devotion to the task of printing them by hand.

Warren L. d'Azevedo

 # *This Herb*

THIS HERB HERE…this Peyote…this little green thing grows in the desert. There ain't no water where It grows, but It's got plenty water in It. When you eat It you ain't thirsty. It fills you up. You ain't hungry.

The whole world is in there. When I am looking at this fine little Peyote here my mind is praying. I can't think of nothing bad. All is good. It shows you everything there is to see…all the people in the world…all the different animals…all the places. It shows you all that's in the sky… everything under this earth here.

With this little Herb you can hear all the Indians in the world singing. You hear their songs and they can hear you. It makes your eyes like x-ray so you can see what's inside things. You can see inside a person and see if he is in good health or he got some sickness in there. It makes your mind like a telegram. You can send your thoughts far away to some other person and that person can send messages to you. It works like electricity. That's why when someone has this Medicine working inside them or when there's a Meeting going on somewhere people can feel It. They know It even if they is twenty miles away. They can hear the songs and feel the people's thoughts.

The Creator put this Herb on Earth for all the people. But Indians is the only ones left know how to use It. Jesus tried to tell the white people how to use It. They forgot, I guess. They eat some kind of bread and drink wine in their church. Maybe they figured that's what He meant. But He meant this Herb…this Medicine. He was just a man like anybody, but the Creator showed Him the way…showed Him where He put the Peyote on the earth for the good of the people. That's why we got Jesus as one of the main Ones in this Indian Tipi Church. We say we have the Peyote, the Creator and Jesus. That's how we believe.

Some white people try to make laws against this Herb. They go against their own life. They don't understand It, so they don't want nobody to have It. But they can't stop It. It grows where the Creator put It. It grows in them Gardens in Texas, in Arizona and all over Mexico. There is millions of Them. Each one of Them little green Herbs is singing His own songs the Creator give Him. Any Indian Member in good standing can hear Them all singing if he go on a run down there to get the Medicine. It is the music the Creator put on this earth to make the mind of humans good and clear. It is for happiness and good health.

The old Indians didn't have no books like the Bible. They didn't have no writing or no books like the white people to read and write what they believe. Indians just think and tell what they believe. But Peyote is like a Bible to us here. Peyote is our Bible. When I'm with this Herb sometimes It is like a book…like turning pages in a book. I want to know something, and I can turn to here, and here, and there. I want to know something else, so I say, 'What is the meaning of that?' And then it is there…everything is in there. It is like that with the Peyote. So I think white people got one kind of book and we got another kind.

When you see this little Herb you see our Church and our Bible. If we keep on the Road It shows us we will have good life. Everything we got to depend on is right here in this Medicine the Creator give us.

 *The Tipi Way*

WHAT THEY CALL the Native American Church, that's the Tipi Way, the Indian Way. It's for all Indians. But it's for another kind of people too if they go that Way honest in peace and good mind.

Now what I heard is every tribe of Indians has some Members in this Church. Every minute, someplace in the world, there is some Members holding Meetings. That keeps the connection going. When we meet in the Tipi, the Medicine leads us along the Path, the real Indian Way. If we do it right...if we sing and pray good and keep our ideas on the Medicine, It connects us with all them other Indians singing and praying all them other places. We can see them just like they was sitting there in our Meeting. All them real Indian men and them fine Indian ladies and little children...they is all working in the same direction, going on that Peyote Road. When you seen that once you can't forget it. Your mind turns around some other way. You ain't the same person again.

This here Church is holding up all Indians. It's the main thing keeps us from being wiped out. There is still plenty people against It, I guess. But all the time there is more starting to understand It. Like in this tribe, here. The Members used to catch a hard time for what they believe. The tribe was all mixed up. Some was trying to be white men and ashamed of the people. Some was just drunk and killing each other. Them old doctors was scared of us...said we was using some kind of power to fool the people. But they was just afraid Peyote was too strong for them. It showed the people how to get protection from the bad ways they was using the old power. In this Tipi Way Church the people get together for the good of everybody. Each person don't work just for himself. He can't use the Medicine just for that. He got to think of his family, all them other ones there in the Tipi…and he got to think good of all the other people in the world, even the ones who is against him.

We don't talk about power like them old doctors do. We just say the Medicine. The Medicine is greater than any of them other things because It was here before any of them. We don't want doctor power. We got the Tipi Way to show us how to help each other and live like real Indians on this fine earth.

Now the people in the tribe see how we live. We don't go round drunk and talking loud. Our kids is in good health. We don't cause no trouble. We don't say we better than anybody else. We just live quiet and do what we think is right. So that's why the people respect us today. Because they see how we respect our own selves. We want to be strong in mind and body like them old Indians a long time ago. We want to live on this earth in peace and good mind with all things the Creator put here.

We take care of everything in the Tipi. That's the meaning of the Tipi Way. We got a special Way of praying in there. When we call a Meeting it is for some reason…not to just sit around. The Members come in there to do something. They got a job to do. They got to keep their mind on it. Somebody is sick or feel bad. We got to help that person. Everyone got to get in on it or the connection won't be good. When we sing and pray with the Medicine everybody got to help. It makes a connection with the Medicine. The Medicine shows the Way and every person there try to get his mind straight so he can get on the Road and do the job. If some person don't do his part he hold back all his friends.

You look at that Tipi outside and it don't look so big. But when you is inside it is like the whole world in there. It's like all the Indians in the world can be in there. You can go out from there and see everything there is. The Members can move around anyplace and see what is happening here and what is going on there. If they is working right they can help someone far away. It's the Medicine does that. If enough people is working right they can make anything happen. I think sometimes if all the Indians was working together there ain't nothing we couldn't do. We could get good life and good health for everyone in this world. They

4

could get a real connection going. I think we could stop people fighting. We could stop a war. We could stop TB and VD and all them things killing people.

But you can't do this just any old way. It's got to be the right Way. In this Tipi things is set up just right. It is the Way we learned from them old Indians...the Way the Medicine showed us. Inside there you got to keep your mind straight so you can help. Everything in there is there for a reason...everything got a meaning. Nobody knows all the reasons for everything. We is learning all the time.

This Tipi got a meaning. It's what them old Indians live in to keep warm and dry. It's got four big poles go up first. That is for the different people in the world. They is tied together at the top because that means they is all One...someday they all going to meet at the top. I heard this from Members in other tribes too. That's what the Medicine shows you. Them poles is the four corners of the world...North, South, East, West. The Tipi always faces East. That is the main direction for us. But each direction got its own meaning. All them other little poles got some meaning too, but I ain't learned about that yet. The canvas we put on there, it means deerskin or buffalo skin or some kind of animal Indians understand from long time ago. We can't deal with them good animals like we used to...so we got to use this canvas.

Inside the Tipi each thing got to have a special place...got to be a special Way. This is a real Church here. When the Tipi go up for a Meeting everything got to be just right. The leader for the Meeting, the Roadchief, goes in there with his helpers and sweep all that ground clean. It's got to be smooth and nice. They do the same thing outside all around the Tipi. Then they go inside fix up the Moon. We use clean sand from the river for that. The open part of the Moon and the points got to face East. You make the top flat and run a line on the Moon from tip to tip. In the middle you make a little mark in the sand. That's where the Roadchief put his own Chief Peyote when the Meeting start. The Peyote Chief is like the Sun and that line on the Moon is like the Sun's path in the sky. That's what I heard.

The Firechief got plenty to do too. He got to cut and stack enough

5

wood to last all night. If he run out it ain't good for the Meeting. It means he ain't too good for that job. He got to keep that Fire going all night. That is our life. The Fire and the Moon and the Chief Peyote sitting there...them is the main things we got to keep our mind on.

The next thing is the drum. The Drumchief got to get ready too. He got to take the drum apart again. You got to start it all over again so it is new for each Meeting. First he untie the skin and wash it good. Then he put new charcoal and fresh water in there. Now he got to tie it up again that special way. You can't play around. It's got to be just right or it won't sound good. When he cinch up the skin each of them seven little rocks got to be in place so the rope on the bottom is just like a star...so it will pull even all around. If he don't know his work it will get loose and mess up somebody's drumming. That drum get plenty action each Meeting. The man who put it together is responsible for that.

The other helpers is the Cedarchief and Watergirl. The Cedarchief got to bring some of that Juniper. We use that to make good smelling smoke in the Meeting. The Indians around here always use that to clean out their house and get rid of sickness. When we put that on the Tipi Fire everybody start to feel better. Sometime we use Sage for that, but we can't get the right kind around here.

Most the time Watergirl is the Roadchief's wife or somebody in his family. She got to be a good lady Member. She got plenty to do too. She's in charge of bringing water at Midnight. Everybody depends on her for that. She got to pray and keep her mind good like sweet water. In the Morning she got to be ready to bring in the real Peyote Breakfast ...only real Indian food like corn and meat and fruit. She pray over that. She pray for it to hold up the life of the people.

When everything is all set the helpers and all the Members come in front of the Tipi. The Roadchief pray for the Meeting and show them how to do...how to make it right. He go in first and sit at the head of the Moon...on the West. Then all the Members follow him. They got to go around on the left side...go around that way. They sit down where they want to. They stay in that place all Meeting. It don't make no diference, except ladies and new Members sit in back if there's a big crowd.

6

The men who is going to sing sit up front around the Fire. But the Roadchief's helpers got to sit special. His Drumchief is on his right side and the Cedarchief is on his left. The Firechief is next to the door so he can get to the wood and keep the floor clean. Watergirl ought to be near there, too, because she got to be ready to do her part.

Every Member in there depends on them helpers. They got to follow the rules if they is going to get anywhere in the Meeting. If they go out, they always got to go around the left way. When they want to pray or get smoke they ask the Chief. Everything passes around that way...one Way. The drum and the songs go around the same Way.

The Medicine pass around that way too. It's up to the Chief to do that. He tells each person to take what they need...what they can handle. It's up to them. But he supposed to know when somebody needs a special treatment. The Roadchief make sure of that...that's his job. He ain't no better than anybody else. He just got that job to do...keep everything going the right Way for that Meeting. He suppose to know something about that. He knows when it's time to start...how to set it up. He knows when it's time for Midnight Water Call and when it's time for Breakfast. He knows the songs and praying for that. He shows the Members the Way to help each other. He keeps his mind on the real reason for that Meeting. He takes care of the Medicine in there.

You can't see nothing better than all them Indian people working in them Meetings. They is all on the Road together. Inside the Tipi they know what they is and what they got to do. There is no strangers in there...no big shots and no little guys. Everybody got the same chance. Everybody is the same kind of Indian if he goes the Tipi Way. When they come out of the Meeting, the new day they see is clean and good. They is strong, and they know what they got to do.

My Outfit

I'M ONE OF THE ONLY GUYS around here who got a complete outfit. It takes a long time to put one together. You don't just go out and buy the stuff. Some guys do that. But that ain't no outfit. It's just a bluff. That kind of outfit can make plenty trouble for you. Each one of them things in there is important. You got to know about it your own self. You can't just take over from somebody else.

I been a Roadchief now about three years. Before that I been in this Church about twenty-five years...ever since I was a kid. All them years I was just learning a little. I still don't know too much. But the people here got some respect for me, I guess. They figure I can help them some. When they started asking me to handle Meetings I wasn't too sure a-bout that. But I got some help from those boys up in Idaho. Seems like my Meetings went okay. Everybody felt pretty good.

I was glad I been working on my outfit by that time. When you run a Meeting you want everything to be the best way...nothing fake...everything the way you learned it.

This here little suitcase got all the main things we need in it. I got the case down in Carson for ten bucks. It ain't too good...made out of some kind of cardboard. But when I get some buckskin big enough I'm going to cover it. Can't use any kind. I want to do the hunting myself so I know it been done right. When you buy that buckskin down in the stores there's no way of telling how it was fixed. It ain't too good to have that kind. It should be fixed the Indian way.

A man ought to go out and do his own hunting and get the things he needs his own self. He don't go out and start shooting. He gets his ideas straight first. He talks to them deer so they know what he got in mind... what he's after. He ain't going out there for fun or to get his limit. He just doing what he got to do to get by. When he shoot one of his brothers out there, he pray. He thank him and tell him not to feel bad against him. That way everything is okay and keeps going on.

There's a certain way you skin him and cut up the meat. Everything is slow and careful so he know you ain't laughing at him. You don't scatter nothing around. When you through you clean up all around there. Any part of him you ain't taking you put in one place under some rocks or something. You treat it careful. Then you talk to him and tell him what you done.

Now that way is okay. When you do that you got the good kind of meat, and the skin is the best. If you tan that skin the Indian way it come out strong and soft and white. That one animal it come from is on your side. He ain't going to make no trouble for you. That's the kind I want on my suitcase. Then my outfit is inside something good.

Here is the main things I got in there. This little box here got my Chiefs in it. When we get a load of Peyote I go through and pick out some of the biggest ones. They is the oldest. Them's the ones you can hear singing sometimes where they grow. This big one here is my special Chief now. When I put him on the Moon I put some sage under him... that's his mattress. I been trying to get my wife to sew some beads on a piece of buckskin for that. She can do it good. I seen a guy from Colorado had his Chief on a mattress like that. It was real pretty. Maybe she do it when she feels like it.

I keep my mind on my Chief button all through a Meeting. Sometimes he tells me something...what I done wrong or how I can get over a tough spot. Sometimes that white hair sticking out of his head there starts to shine so bright it hurts my eyes. Like the sun. It gets bigger and bigger until everything is bright like daytime. I can see right out of the Tipi and all around. I can see everything going on.

Some guys say they eat their Chief button when they got to have special help. I never did that. When they get dried up I put them in this little tin box where I keep the new Chief I'm using. That way the old ones see what's going on and help the new Chief along.

I got two fans here. They is eagle feathers. I just started using eagle a couple years ago. I'm old enough now, I think. It ain't good to use them if you is too young. This one here I use myself. The feathers is kind of worn out and it ain't got so fancy beadwork and jewels like the other one there. But it's the one give me by the guy who showed me how to run Meetings. He come down from Idaho to give us a hand. He been using this fan a long time. He got it from somebody straightened him out in South Dakota. So I use it when I'm working.

This here other fan is real pretty. Each of them feathers is sewed on with its own buckskin blanket and beads. One of the Members here made that for me. He did it pretty good. I use that one to send around the Tipi with the cane for the ones who is singing.

I got a cane here I made myself out of that mountain mahogany. It got a screw part here in the middle so I can take it down and fit it in my outfit. Some guys put some kind of hair or feathers on top of theirs, and sew beads all around. But I heard this cane is for business. It's got to be strong to hold you up when you is on the Road. It don't need all that stuff on it.

These rattles I had for a long time. This one here was made by a guy used to come to Meetings up from Bridgeport. He did a pretty good job. Them is hummingbird feathers on top of the gourd. Them beads on the handle is fixed just like I saw on some old rattles. The colors go right up from dark circles to bright ones…like the Meetings…from Night to Morning. And the feathers up there is Sunrise. These two here ain't so fancy. But they been around. I got them from a Member when I first started to come to Meetings. He said they come from some old Member in Utah. Them is real old gourds. They sound clear…plenty songs in them. I like to use that kind.

This basket here…that's a real good Washoe basket. My wife made that. She put all them beads all over it, too. Not many women around can make this kind no more. She made this top for it the same way. I keep some special things in there. Here's my whistle. Not many guys got one out of real eagle leg bone like this one. It sounds real good when I start the Meeting and when I go outside for Midnight. My friend in Idaho give me this.

10

I keep this little bag of Sage in here, too. This is different from the Sage we got around here. It's got flat leaf and smell strong. I mix it with tobacco I give the Members for smoke. Sometimes I put a little on the fire. But I go easy on it. It come from way back east somewhere. I got Bull Durham here for smokes. I don't like nobody to smoke them white cigarettes in the Meetings. This here Bull Durham is like real Indian tobacco. You got to roll your own in this here brown paper. That's the way I learned it. So I always keep some of that in here for the Members.

These badges here is real silver. This one here is Waterbird and this one is the Moon. There was a guy in Smith Valley used to make these out of dollars. You see some guys still got some. I put them on when I go to Meeting.

I got some Stars in this matchbox. When I find any good little glass rocks or beads or brass balls I keep them in there. That's if any fall out of my gourd. They got to be the right size and just the right kind to sound good. There's got to be seven Stars in there or the rattle sound bad some kind of way. It spoil your song.

This little blanket I keep here to lay out my outfit at the Meeting. I got that in Arizona one time. It come from Mexico, I think. I put that down in front of me and then each thing I need at the Meeting goes on it just the right place. That way they keep clean and everybody can see what I got. They know I ain't holding nothing back...everything is out in the open.

I got a bunch of extra drumsticks in here...each one a little different ...maybe heavy one way, or longer...different kind of way it feel. Sometime you like to change to a different one. In the Meeting a guy might want to have a different stick. I want to be ready for something like that.

My drum is kind of heavy to go in with them other things. I keep it in this here sack when I ain't using it. I got the skin in there and the rope and them small rocks for tying it up...everything all ready to go when I need it. That pot is the good old kind. Them miners used to get them around here. They got little legs and the iron is the strong kind sounds like a bell when you tap it. You can't find them much no more. One guy wants to pay me fifty bucks for it. But he can't never pay for all the

Meetings that drum been in. I tell him go find some white man find him a drum.

Only one thing I need now for a whole outfit. I been trying to get a big Tipi. I been using one my friends keep down there in the river camp. It's pretty old and the canvas full of holes. There's a place down in Reno makes good Tipis. The big kind I want is about one hundred bucks. I can't quite make it. But one of these days I'm going down and talk to them. Maybe they let me pay a little at a time. If I had my own Tipi I could set up a Meeting anywheres. The people just need to have the poles cut. Sometimes I go someplace people don't have no Tipi. We got to meet out in the open or in somebody's house. This way I can bring my Tipi to them people. There ain't many Tipis around in this part of the country...maybe three or four. Most of them is too small.

But this here is about everything I need for Meeting. I can pack this up and go anyplace someone wants to set up Meeting. I got to be ready to move around. That bunch down in Bridgeport sends word, I got to be ready. Some people down in California say they need a Chief, I got to get down there. Anybody around here call for a Meeting, I can't turn them down if they need it. Even if I been working all day on the job, I got to go. I just take some Medicine so I feel strong again. Then I go over to the hot spring to clean up and pray a little. That puts me in shape so I can work all night. Sometimes if someone is real sick I got to carry that Meeting over two or three nights. I got to keep in shape for that.

The main thing about being a Roadchief is keeping your own body and mind straight. If you is sick or got something on your mind it ain't good for the people. The other main thing is having your outfit just right. All them things is your own responsibility. You got to know what you doing with each thing. You got to know how it works...you got to be able to trust it. It can't be nothing you just picked up somewhere. You got to know its ways and it got to know you.

If you make any kind of mistake in there it is up to you. Maybe somebody die in there, or some kind of sickness or a bad idea gets away from you. Then you is in real trouble with the people and they don't want you coming around again. The Medicine will kick you hard when that happens. It shows you how you ain't ready and you got to take time to straighten out. When that happens you check yourself out real good. You check out your outfit and see if there's anything in there giving trouble. You can't take chances. This Medicine is good but you can't play with it. It keeps pushing you to go the right Way. If you can't do it, you got no business trying to be a leader with It.

The Medicine is the main thing of all. It's our life. None of them other things here can do much without the Herb the Creator give us. That's something else a Roadchief got to deal with. It don't make much difference what kind of outfit he got if there ain't no Medicine for the people. Right now we running kind of short around here. We just got a little bit of the dry buttons left. A couple a weeks ago I got some of the fresh green ones from some of my friends over in California. But them's all gone now.

I could send for some, I guess. We do that sometimes. There's that place in Mirando City in Texas don't cost too much. He got the dried buttons and the ground up kind...any kind you want. You can get green ones, too. You send some money, they ship it to you. But sometimes you don't get good ones, or they short you. Besides, we don't like the Post Office to look in there. It ain't a good idea if they check on that. The best way is to go find the Herb yourself. That way you know what you got. You really doing something then.

So maybe somebody got to make a run down to Texas. Most of the Members is pretty broke right now. If I can get a couple of tires and fix the radiator maybe my car can make it. It's my job if nobody else can do it. Maybe I'll take my wife and kids. They ain't seen that Indian country down there. Anyway, somebody got to do it.

 *Songs*

THE WAY A MAN SING shows you what kind of person he is. If he sings good, he can help people. His song goes through them and the Medicine is working. Singing is like praying... it's the same thing. When we sing here it is for a reason. That's the Indian way.

A song ain't just to play with. It's for a reason. It comes out of the mind. If you got good thoughts that song comes out of your body clear and strong. It's like praying... like the Cedar Smoke. The drum and the rattle carry the song out to everything. The song goes into things... into people... straightens them out. The vibration in there changes things around so they can get a good connection... like praying... like when the feathers in your fan is full of Cedar Smoke and you switch that good Smoke into a person and they feel cleaned out and good.

All the songs we sing in this Church here is good. There ain't no bad songs unless a person is thinking bad. Maybe some songs sound better, or a person is a better singer than somebody else. But that don't make any difference about the song. It depends upon the person and his thoughts. You can tell that.

A person has to do his best. I try to sing a song just the way I heard it. I try to get it just right. It's hard work to sing it right. It takes a long breath. These here Peyote songs is different from our old Washoe songs. Them old songs is slow. But Peyote songs is fast and you got to carry your voice way up high and then down low. That is different from old Washoe songs. So we learn to sing them songs just the way we heard them.

Sometimes a song don't come out right. Your mind ain't ready for it yet. Something catches in your throat like a hand choking you. That means the Medicine is showing you ain't ready...or maybe something ain't right and getting in your way. You better pray and wait to get cleared up. There was that Member here trying to get his songs put on a tape recorder. When he was finished singing there wasn't nothing on the tape. Maybe that machine didn't want his songs. Maybe the Medicine won't let them songs get taken down...something was wrong. That guy didn't have his mind right. It's the same way when you run out of breath on a song. That means you ain't ready. You got to wait and get strong.

Some Members sing any song they know any time in the Meeting. That's okay, so long as he's doing his best. But there is certain songs for for each part of the Meeting...certain songs for Starting, for Midnight, for Morning and for Quitting. When you learn them that way you should sing them in the right place. They got a chance to work better if you do it the right Way of the Church. But that's up to the person and what he knows. We don't like to be too strict here. We take it easy and give a person a chance. Any song is good if the person is doing the best they can. But a Roadchief ought to have his songs right. He's got to know the special songs for different times of the Meeting. That's his job.

We don't believe like some Church Members do in some other tribes. They say you got to do things a certain way or they won't let you in their Meeting. If you just come to pray or sing the songs you know, they say 'No, you got to do it one way'. They act like you ain't a good Member. We don't believe in that here. Anybody want to come in our Meeting here and do some good for himself or other people can come in anytime. That's the easy way. Ben Lancaster started that. When he first come here nobody knew any real Church songs. Lot of them didn't even know any old Indian songs. So Ben started to ask people to sing any songs they know...Indian songs, Hillbilly songs, Gospel songs. They could sing any kind of song so long as they mean business. Later on they began to learn the real Peyote songs. Them is the best ones to sing in the Meeting. But we don't stop a person from singing the song he knows. He just got to make sure he sing it four times. That number four is important in there. If someone forget that, we try to set him straight on that.

Another thing Ben did when he got this Church started here was let ladies sing. I guess he did that because the ladies was his best helpers when he was getting started. He kind of liked the ladies, I guess. But we learned that wasn't the Way. Only men supposed to do the singing. The ladies can pray and help out singing with them a little. But the man carries the song. That is a rule. We go by that here, now. The ladies is real important in the Church. You can't have no Meeting without them. The men can't go it alone. That lady's got to pray on the Water, and the ladies fix the Breakfast. They can pray good too. If a man don't have a woman on his side he's in trouble.

Sometimes the women help you when you is singing. That's when you sing real good. The ladies in the Meeting start praying in a high voice along with your song. That's real good when it happens. It makes the song travel out straight and clear. If you get helpers like that it means your song is going pretty good.

The guy who's drumming for you is your main helper in there. If he's too fast or too slow he can spoil your song. You can tell about a man that way... if he is your friend or if he has his mind straight. The best way is to have somebody drum for your songs you know a long time and you trust him. The drummer is supposed to follow you, but he carries you too. The drum carries the song out. It's got to be tied just right and the water and coals in there got to shake right. The drummer got to shake the drum now and then to keep the skin wet...that changes the sound of his beat. He can blow on the skin to get air in there and make that deep sound. He got to know how to move his thumb around on top of the drum. It's a gift. When the Medicine gives you the gift to use the drum right It goes through the body and then you can help. You can't learn in five years...you just keep trying until It comes to you. If you pray good, the Supreme Master may hear you and will help you to drum good. When you is singing with a friend who drums good your songs is better than they ever sounded before.

Your rattle is just as important as the drumming. You got to have a gourd with just the sound to fit your voice. Each guy figures that out for himself. You got to try plenty of gourds before you find the right one.

When you find the sound you know it by the way it goes with your songs. When the sound is right it seems like you ain't shaking the rattle. It's like your hand ain't moving and the rattle is shaking itself. It's the same way when the drum is right. The drumstick goes by itself.

That shaking sound you hear sometimes in the Tipi is the Medicine working...not just the man singing does that...the Medicine and good thoughts do that. It means everything is just right. It means you are making a connection in there. It makes the tent poles wobble. That's good. The Meeting is on the Road then. Everybody is going the right Way then. Old men who been going to Meetings a long time...good men...they can start that sound going. They got that real Indian sound in their voice. The Medicine helps that along.

We say all songs is good if a person is out to do good with them. But these here Peyote songs...these Church songs...is the best songs we got in this Tipi Way. They come from way back. They been tried out by them Indians all over for a long time. It's best to use them in there. We don't have to know what them words mean. They ain't like ordinary words. Maybe they from some language of another tribe. Maybe they from language people a long time ago speak on this earth, or maybe it is from someplace we don't know about. We don't worry about that. We just learn them songs and sing them the way we hear them. That way you know you ain't going wrong.

I don't know all the meaning of my songs. I don't try to figure what them words mean. Plenty old Indian songs like that. I just try to sing them good. I just know my own feelings. I just sing the songs like a tune...it carries my thoughts out. Some songs have a happy sound. Some songs got sad kind of sounds. But that's just the way you feel about them when you hear them and sing them. You know what it means, that's all. You don't have to talk about it. You know when a song is good.

Sometimes you put words of your own language in the song if it fits there. The Shoshonis and Paiutes do that a lot. But the Washoe language is too slow...the words that got the right meaning is too long to fit in. But it's okay to try to do that if you want to. It's okay to change the song

17

a little. Then you can understand something special in there. Sometimes songs got English words in them...like 'Jesus only one', or 'Jesus coming now'. Well, that's all right. They put that in there because some people got Jesus on their mind. That's okay too.

Some guys got a special song of their own...they like to sing it special. Maybe they only got two or three songs and they sing them all the time. They sing each song over four times in the Meeting and they sing that same bunch all night. They say them songs is the right ones for them. It's okay if that's what they want to do. Other guys like to learn a lot of songs so they can go a whole Meeting not singing the same one again. Each man is different the way he wants to go. It depends on him ...just as long as he is honest in his own mind.

There is some people say they can catch songs...they hear it and it comes right into them so they can sing it the first time. That happened to me once so I know it is so. I heard that song once and then it was like it was all there in my head. I started singing it just like I been working on it a long time. It is one of my main songs. I sing it when I need special help. It always turns out right. The man I heard it from was my good friend up in Fort Hall. He sung it for me once when I wasn't in too good shape. He gave me seven little green buttons and sung that song. I felt good right away and that song went into my head and came out of my throat. I never had no trouble with it...just sang it right out. It's been a kind of special kind of song for me ever since.

Sometimes a person can hear a song in their head they never heard before. They catch it right away and can sing it. That never happened to me, but I know it can happen because there's some guys never been nowhere and can't sing many songs, but all of a sudden right there while you is listening they come out with a new song you never heard. They say it just come to them. It pushes out of them and they got to sing it. That kind of song is pretty good. It means the Medicine is helping that person along. I like to hear that kind...if you trust the person singing it. You can really understand that person when he is singing it.

I pay attention to the way each man sings. I know all about a person the way he sings. When I sing, each song is like part of my own self. It can't be no better than me. So when I sing, it ain't like on the radio or to pass the time. I'm trying to get myself up as good as I can. I don't just sing a song…I'm taking a trip. When I'm singing I'm praying in the Tipi and going on that trip over that Road.

 *Creation*

SOME INDIANS around here say it was Coyote made people. But that's just some kind of old story. They heard that from old time people. Maybe they believe everything they hear is true. That's okay if they want to do that but it don't mean it's true. Them old people think Coyote was the big shot around here in the old old days. But them old stories don't mean like that. They just something you tell the kids to put them to sleep or when people sitting around having fun.

The way I heard it from Indians in this Church is different. They don't talk about Coyote or Wolf or all them other animals running around here doing them things. They got no time for that kind of business. They want to get the facts.

The way I heard it the Creator made man…what we call Detumu, the leader, the highest One, Supreme. This is what they call the God. The God wanted to make people. So he gathered up some dirt and clay and made it into the image of a person. He took it over into the sun so He could bake it. He was trying to make Indians…redskins. But that first clay He made didn't turn out right...wasn't cooked enough. It made a white skin. Well, I guess He think that was okay too, so He breathed His life into it and made it into a person. Then He put that one aside and tried another one. He was still trying to make an Indian.

So He made that other one and put it into the sun to bake. He left it there a little longer. But it was kind of yellow skin. So that was made, and He breathed His life into it and put it with the other one. There was the white and yellow now.

But He was still thinking about the other one...the redskin. So He put another one out...the image of a man in clay. He put it out there in the sun to bake a little more. But He left it there a little too long. It turned a little bit too dark...burnt a little too much. So, anyway, that one was there, so He let that one come to life...breathed His life into it and then He put it over there with the others.

So He was going to try one more. This time He would fix it just right ...just the color the way He wanted...with red skin...the one He wanted to make in the first place. It came out okay. It was good.

He said, 'Now this is the one that is good I wanted to make'. So He breathed His life into it and made it come alive and put it along with the rest of them. So now He had to figure where they was going to live. So He put the white ones way over there, and the yellow ones way over there, and the black ones He put way over there where it is warm. The Indians was right here where they are living now in different places. The God gave them the power to have kids and to generate different nationalities like they is today.

That's how I heard it from the people. It sounds right to me because that could happen. There's that story about the God making only one man and then He made a woman from a rib out of the man. It don't make much sense to me. What's He got to hurt that man for? He can make anything He wants to. That's a white people's story. Maybe it happened too. But it don't explain much. It only explains one kind of people...the white people. This other story explain the four different kind of people in the world. It sounds like the real one to me.

Now the number four is in there. There is four in everything. Four corners of the earth, we say. You have to have four to make things come out right. Just like in the Meetings, you have four of everything...four things to start with. And the Tipi's got four poles...main poles. Those four main poles to hold it up stand for the four different people in the world and the four directions of the world. They come together at the top and they stand for all the people of the world and how they are all going to end up the same place...all come together. Some day they will all come together...one kind of people...one place. But that won't happen in our time. That is way off...a long time from now.

Feathers

ONE OF THE FINEST things in the world is feathers. Sometimes they is so pretty you can't believe they just grew that way out of a bird. You want to look at them all the time. When you put them all together in a fine fan, each one bound with buckskin on a handle with fancy bead-work, you think you are looking at all the sunrises in the world at the same time.

But you got to be careful with feathers. Each one got its own special ways and its own kind of power. Each one belongs to that bird it came from and you can't forget that. You can't play around with feathers like they was nothing. You have to know how to handle them. A man has to know what is best for him and what he can deal with. If he tries to take on too much or go too fast he can get hurt.

Like Eagle. You got to take it easy with eagle feathers. Some guys act like eagle feathers is for anybody. But that ain't right. You got to be ready for them. Even if a guy is a Roadchief it don't mean he should use them. You got to be clear about that. If you been in this Church a long time, the Medicine lets you know about that. Once we had a Roadchief here who got some eagle feathers and wanted to make himself a real Chief fan. He put two of them feathers between his teeth while he was bind-ing them. But he turned them the wrong way and they knocked out his two front teeth. You got to turn them clockwise, but he turned them the other way. He wasn't ready for them. So he put them away until he learns all that. But even then he may not be ready. Not everyone can use them.

Maybe there was something wrong the way them feathers was got.

You can't just go kill an eagle. That kind will work against you. You have to get them in some way that eagle don't mind. Maybe that eagle will drop one sometime, and you can just pick it up. You thank the eagle for that. Sometimes you find one dead. You can take them feathers as long as you pray to the eagle and let him know you didn't have nothing to do with him dying. In the old days some Indians around here knew where eagles made their nest way up on the rocks. Well, if they was careful and knew their business they could go up there and find feathers all around. But if you didn't know how to talk to them eagles maybe you didn't come down from there. I heard there was certain guys in the old days that could go up and catch eagles and pull out a couple of their feathers. But they had to be pretty strong guys with special ways. Maybe they was war guys or some kind of doctors. I never heard of nobody doing that these days.

I don't mess around with eagle feathers. One time somebody gave me a bunch of different kind. There was two big long black ones he said came from some kind of eagle in Mexico. There was some brown ones with sort of red and white edges. And there was some of the yellow and brown kind like the eagles around here. But I didn't want to touch any of them. They was all real shiny and strong looking. I told that guy to take them back, because I didn't know where they come from and they might be from some kind of buzzard or something. He said he didn't know too much about them either. I don't know what he did with them, but I never seen him with any of them in his fans. I don't know why he was trying to give them to me.

I don't like to mess with loon or owl or hawk either. They don't seem right for me. But some guys try them. I like to get all kind of different color feathers from other birds. I use pheasant, sagehen, parrot. Sometimes I get them little hummingbird feathers. I like my fan to have bright colors. I been trying to get some of them peacock feathers, but I never found how to get them yet. Sometimes when I go down to San Francisco I go out to that place they keep all them animals. There is a place there with nothing but birds from all over the world. They got some real pretty ones. Sometimes feathers drop down to the ground and you can reach in and pick them up. But they don't like you to do that around there, and I got run off one time. There was a guy who worked there one time, though, and he used to save the feathers for me when he cleaned the cages. I got a lot from him. But then he stopped working there and I ain't had much luck since.

I tried to get some feathers off of them peacocks they got running around there. But them birds is pretty smart, and you can't get close enough to grab one. I don't think they would even feel it if you pulled out just one. I used to follow them around to see if they ever dropped any. I talked to them a little. But it didn't do no good. I never got any.

Some guys like to use only one kind of feathers in their fans. They say you got to use just one kind in the fan so when you spread it out or point it you can sight along that fan and see clear and fly like that bird them feathers come from. They say if you use too many different kinds the fan is going to look like a bunch of chicken feathers and your mind is going to start running around and clucking like a chicken when you use the fan. Well, that's their way, I guess. That's all right, too. But I got one good fan with all kinds of bright colored feathers and different sizes. When I spread it out or point it I feel like I am pulling all good things in the world together...all them fine bright things birds see when they are flying far away in other places. But I'm careful about which feathers I use. I don't just take any just because I found it. I think about them for a while, and I take some Medicine and look at them. Sometimes there's one feather that don't look right. It was pretty when I found it, but when I start looking at it strong it turns some bad way and I don't want to touch it again. Maybe that feather come from some kind of bird I can't deal with, or maybe that bird it come from got some bad idea in it for some reason. You got to be careful about that or you going to have some kind of trouble with your fan. If you don't know what you are doing you are always in danger. But that is why you have to depend on the Medicine. It can show you.

The feathers I like best is magpie. I got one special fan made from just magpie tailfeathers. Everybody sees it and knows it is my own fan and them feathers are for me some way. They are shiny black like the sky when there ain't no moon, and you can see little stars in them. I only use that fan sometimes when I am feeling just right. It took me a long time to get all them feathers. I keep a lookout for them all the time when I'm walking around. Them old Washoe Indians around here say the people liked to use magpie in the old days. Them fighting guys put one feather sticking up out of their hair when they went to war. They was tough guys and that was their way.

Them magpies is tough. Even big birds and animals don't bother them. I seen them chasing dogs and hawks away from their food. They are plenty smart, too. When you ain't trying to hunt them they come around like chickens. But when you are after their feathers, they know it, and you can't get close to them. When I been eating the Medicine they come so close to me sometimes I have to shoo them away. They know I'm not supposed to kill or bother anything when I am with the Medicine.

But one time I was sitting under that tree outside my place. Four big magpies was hopping around close to me and looking at me kind of sly. If I moved they made a racket and flew away a little bit. So I didn't move. I just sat there looking at them and keeping friendly ideas in my head. They come real close acting like they didn't know I was there. Then the biggest one started poking around and cleaning himself like they do. The other ones start doing the same. Then each one pulled out a big tail feather and dropped it right there on the ground. I saw them do that. The feathers just didn't drop off. They was pulled out. Then they made a big racket like they was laughing at me and flew up in the tree. Well, I didn't make one move. I just look up and watch them like I am in no hurry about nothing. They kept making a big racket waiting for me to make my move. But when they saw I wasn't no plain dumb Indian ready to play their game, they flew away after a while. If I look too interested and grab them feathers right away they would still be laughing at me. They are mean guys in some ways, and like to make you look dumb.

But I just sat there quiet for a long time. I took a little Medicine and and prayed a little to them feathers. They looked good, the finest ones I ever seen. I sang a song in my head until I felt pretty good. Then I picked up the feathers and spread them out like a fan. I sang a little more and then took them into the house. Them same birds came back later and sat in the tree for a couple of hours. They didn't make no noise... just sat there keeping an eye on things. I never saw them four birds again after that day, but it seems like I can find good magpie feathers laying on the ground wherever I go. When someone wants that kind of feather they come to me for them.

Another thing I noticed since that time. Magpies don't make a racket when they come around me. If I come around, they get quiet. Everyone notices that.

Two Friends

THERE WAS TWO INDIANS in Oklahoma...in that place there ...around Tulsa, I think. They was friends for a long time, ever since they was small boys. And when they was grown up they went to school and then to college. They was just like white men. Them two guys knew about Indians taking that Medicine, that Herb. They said that anybody eat that Peyote is crazy and it was bad for the Indians to do that.

Them two friends made a promise that they would never go to them Meetings or eat that Peyote. They said they would do everything they could to change that and to stop them Indians from going that way.

Then the two friends didn't see each other for a long time and they had to go work in different places.

It was a long time after that one of them guys was in Kansas, and he got sick and he almost died right then. He went to white doctors and they tell him he has something no medicine is invented to cure. They tell him that he might die from that disease. And he felt so bad he didn't know what to do.

Then somebody told him some of them Indians was holding Meetings over there and trying to do good and help people out who was sick. He felt so bad he forgot all about his promise and he decided to go there. He went to one of them Meetings and he saw lots of Indians there all eating that Medicine and singing and praying. He eat some of that and he prayed and they prayed for him and he felt better a little. He kept going to them Meetings, and pretty soon he is in good health again even though them white doctors say he will die.

He started believing and doing that Way. He was sorry he never thought about his own people all that time he was trying to live the white way. He let his hair grow out long and he lived the Indian way.

A long time after that the other friend was in Kansas and he heard about the Meetings. He thinks maybe he will go there just to see what it is like. He went to that Meeting there and he saw all them Indians sitting around that fire in the Tipi. And he was surprised to hear all the Indians singing those good songs and living in the old Indian way. He began to feel sad about the way he been thinking about them people. He took some of that Medicine and It made him feel better.

All the time he was sitting next to his friend. But he didn't know his friend. Finally he looked at this man next to him and he say, 'I think maybe I know you sometime...I think I know you somewhere.' And his friend say, 'Yes, I am your friend for so long. We used to go to school together. Remember when we promised not ever to go here like this? But now we are both here.'

Then the other man says, 'Now I remember you. You are my friend that I don't see for so long!'

And he look at his friend who had long hair like Indians now, and who was in good health and knew the Indian way. And he stay there with his friend that way.

 *Stranger In the Tribe*

WE GOT A NEW MEMBER who been living around here with us for a while now. He's sitting right over there. You all know him. He got married to that young girl, my cousin from around Minden. We know he has been trying to get along here. I don't know of any trouble he got into with the people around here since he been here. He come all the way from Ute country to live here and settle down. He don't speak our language, so sometimes people talk Washoe when he's around, and sometimes people seem sort of avoiding him. It seems to him sometimes people don't want him around.

Well, he comes to me and says he wants me to speak for him to the people here. He says he wants me to tell the people he come to stay here with us because he like the ways here and he like this good clean country in the mountains. He says he been to meetings before in his own tribe and he has lived in other tribes too. He says some of them other tribes don't have much use for the Washoe...say they are kind of hard to get along with...to keep to themselves. But he says he seen more trouble in them other tribes than he ever seen here. People was easy going here and didn't bother you too much. So he got married and set himself down here. When he says these Washoe people here, he means the Members right around here and them that comes to these Meetings. He says he can't get along with them other people. There's too much drinking and and fighting and they don't want to make you feel at home.

Well, this Member says everything has been going alright for a while. Nobody treat him bad. But he says he's been here for a while now and he still feels like he is a stranger from another tribe. People don't talk to him much and nobody comes by his place to say hello. Even some of his wife's close family don't seem to come around much. He says he feels lonesome sometimes. He thinks maybe people talking about him and got something against him.

Well, I told him, 'Don't worry too much about that. People here is good people. They got nothing against you. They just got to get used to you for a while more.' I tell him he ain't the only one has trouble like that. I know some Washoe people around here that feels lonesome in their own tribe...just like they was a stranger in their own tribe. That's because the people don't always live by the good idea we got in this Church here. The Medicine tells us that anybody trying to live right and follow this Peyote Way is like our own close family. We got no strangers in this Tipi.

Some people forget that sometimes. You can't think about different tribes and different color people in this Church. We got to work with the new Way, now. This is the new Indian Way...the New Tipi Way. It is for all people who want to come here in peace and good mind. We don't keep nobody away. If they are good people they are like our own brothers and sisters.

So I told him this. And I told him about that old sort of warchief we heard about who used to live up there in Long Valley by Honey Lake. He was part Washoe and part Paiute. He felt like he belonged to both tribes. But there was lots of trouble between the tribes in those days. There was lots of trouble with the whitemen coming in, too. When the Washoes had trouble with the Maidus, that old chief would lead them against that tribe. If the Paiutes had trouble with the Maidus or Pitt Rivers, he would help the Paiutes. If any Indians had trouble with the whitemen, he helped them. But when there was trouble between the Paiutes and the Washoes, he didn't know which way to go. He got all mixed up, and felt like he couldn't go against any of his relatives.

That old man was thinking about that. After he been thinking about it for a long time he began to think that fighting and killing was the wrong way. He didn't think it was right for Indians to kill Indians, and he even started thinking it wasn't right to kill anybody else either. He began talking against fighting and said people should all live like close relatives together.

Well, that man had trouble just like some of us do. People started laughing at him. Some people didn't have nothing to do with him no more. Some people got real mad at him and tried to make him go away. Even his own family sort of left him alone. He wasn't any kind of war-chief no more and he was just an old man by himself.

But that old man had a good idea. If he was around here in these days he would know how to teach us to be real Members of this Church.

So when my brother, here, come to me, I told him this. And I told him not to worry none. Give these people here a chance, I say.

Jesus and the Donkey

THERE WAS A MAN once making believe he was Jesus Christ. A Kiowa, I think, back east somewhere. This really happened, I heard. One time this man came to the people over there, telling them, 'I'm Jesus Christ. That's me. I'm the guy now. I'm the guy you are praying to all the time. You people gather over there in that field there. I'm going to come there at a certain time. You people gather over there and bring flowers and lay them in my path. You people get ready for me to come, and kneel down. I'll be coming on my donkey.

Well, them people believe it, I think. They said, 'We'll see you that time.'

Next morning all the people was there waiting for him. They seen him coming over there riding on his donkey. They all kneeled down to see Jesus Christ himself. Some of them put the flowers down all around so he could walk on them. And when he was coming closer everyone there kneel down closing their eyes so they could think about Jesus coming.

There was one little boy there sharpening his stick. This boy look around if anyone was watching him. When Jesus and his donkey come close that little boy poke the donkey in the hind end. That donkey jump and run right out from under Jesus Christ. Jesus Christ started cussing and chasing that boy around.

The people looked up and said, 'What's the matter now? That Jesus is cussing around. What kind of Jesus Christ is that?'

But one of those guys said, 'Don't get excited, people. Jesus Christ don't say like that. That's only one mistake he made there. He never said like that before. That's the first time he ever say it. That's the first mistake he ever made.'

So the people didn't say nothing more.

Sometime, way after that, this same guy was going to come along again. He was going to preach to the people about the Bible and all that. He had his donkey tied up to a post by a long rope. He was talking to them people.

That same little boy was there. He started to yell, 'Hey, people, there's a big fire over there!'

Everybody started running to put out the fire. Jesus Christ started running too. He jumped on his donkey. The donkey ran so far as the end of that rope. And that Jesus kept going and fell right over the donkey's head.

Them people said, 'That guy is no Jesus.'

So that guy went home and shaved off his whiskers and came back to the people just like one of them.

The idea in there is not to make believe a person is Jesus. If you make that kind of mistake people won't believe you no more.

The Indian Doctor
& the Peyote Chief

SOME INDIANS came out here from back East once. They told me this story to show how you better not fool around with the Medicine.

One time an Indian doctor came to one of their Meetings. They have real Meetings back there, they say, with real buckskin Tipi and a fine white Moon in the center and the right kind of Sage and Cedar. This Indian doctor come and said he wanted to come into their Tipi and see what they are doing with that Medicine. The Roadchief of them people didn't say nothing, but he wondered about that. He knew them Indian doctors got different medicines for power. They have old time ways and are full of tricks. They don't care about the people…they just want to show their power. They don't understand the Medicine we use for the good of the people.

Well, that Indian doctor came into that Meeting. All the people was there sitting around the Moon. When the Roadchief put his Peyote Chief on the Moon and began to pray to his Chief, the Indian doctor just laughed.

He said, 'Watch what I will do!' Then he stared at the fine Peyote Chief on the Moon. He shook his head back and forth and rolled it a-round while he was staring at the Chief. Then, all of a sudden, that fine big Chief button stood up on end and began to roll like a coin around the Fire. Then It rolled toward the doctor, right up his leg and into his shirt pocket. When that happened the doctor laughed at the Members.

The Roadchief began to cry and begged the doctor to put his Chief back on the Moon. But the doctor just laughed and said, 'I can make your medicine do tricks for me!'

Then the Roadchief said very sad, 'You have been invited here as a friend and yet you have done this. You are making fun of our Medicine and treating It with no respect. You have made us ashamed. I beg you to put It back where It was. It is for our health and our life. If you have any love for your health and life I beg you to put It back. I can't punish you, but my Chief knows what to do.'

But the Indian doctor only laughed and went away. Two years later, he got paralyzed. He couldn't walk. For the rest of his life the only way he could get around was by rolling over and over where he wanted to go. He had to roll round and round just like he had made the Medicine do.

 *Praying*

HOW CAN AN INDIAN pray like a white man? The white man gets his prayers out of books...old books about things maybe thousands of years ago. He don't even have to think about it. He just says it and it is supposed to do him some good. He can be a drunk bum for a long time, do all kinds of no good thing, think all kinds of bad thoughts about people. But then he can walk right into that Church and pray one of them prayers and he gets away with it. Anybody can go into them Churches anytime and walk out without anything happening to him.

But Indians here don't have no books, and they don't think about things a long time ago. We just have our own mind and own thoughts, and we think about what happened today among the people. We are thinking about what is right there before us, what happened in the daylight when this sun was shining today and people was just going around doing what they have to do every day. We think about that, and what kind of a person we been that day. We just think what is in our mind at that time...what kind of shape we is in. We don't have any old books to tell us old things. We want to know about new things that are happening today. We want to hear about this sun and this earth and these people right here. That's what counts and that's what we are up against. That's what we got to work with. That's all we got. We want to do something about that.

It's hard for an Indian to pray. He don't have a prayer given to him to say. He has to think of it himself. It has to be right out of his own mind. He has to think about it a long time. It has to be right. If he ain't right or the words ain't right, they can kick back at him. Sometimes the words just don't come, because there is something holding them back. It don't do no good to just make something up. You just can't say it if you don't feel it right. The words don't come. If you just say anything to sound good, you might hurt somebody, or it might come back and hit you hard. You have to sit there and wait for it to come right out of your own body. Maybe it don't come. Then you know something is really wrong inside. You can't force it out. You just have to try to live right and then maybe it will come out of you some other time.

A man has a lot of feeling inside him...more than he can ever get hold of all at once. You have to wait and work for it by the way you think and live. It comes with singing and with praying and living right. You have to work hard for a long time...clean your mind. You have to keep your mind on good things...on other people and what you want good for them. You have to think about your own life and how you want to be. Then you will feel that feeling coming inside of you. It is like you will cry. A grown man can't cry unless he is hurt bad. Well, it's like that... like you are hurt bad. Like you feel sorry for yourself, how no good you are, and how you haven't done anything good for yourself or anyone. The feeling just starts coming out of your body. You can't help it. The words come with it. The words come right out of the body. Then you start talking good like you never did talk before. You feel strong and good like a real man. Then you feel strong enough to help other people along a bit. That's what real Indian praying is. It's a connection...a real connection with something. You don't just think about yourself any more. You don't worry about them things. You are thinking about big good things.

Sometimes it is a long time before it comes again. Sometimes you just can't feel anything strong. But you have to work at it hard. That's what those Indians mean about praying.

An Indian can't go into his Church the same way as a white man. When you go into that Peyote Meeting, you don't just go there for a visit. You go there to work, and if you got something on your mind that isn't right, well, that is something to worry about. That Peyote ain't easy on you like that Bible is. Jesus was living thousands of years ago, but that Peyote is living right now. It is growing right now, and it will be hard on you if you ain't ready for It. They say Jesus died and came to life again. That Jesus was a good man, they say. He was just a man like us. But Peyote was always there. It can kill you or bring you life. It all depends on you. The minute you take that Peyote It is working on you and finding you out.

That's the way Indians always thought. Sometimes you have to pay for what you done. You might say something or do something and think you will get away with it. But you can't. Sometime...maybe a long time from now...when you forgot all about what you said or did, you will get it all back. Peyote makes you think of that. It is hard on you if you ain't in shape. It makes you pay. It makes you think about everything. It shows you what you got to do. You can't get by...you can't fool It. If you try, you will have a worse time.

Sometimes It is too much for a person who is just starting. He quits because he can't face It. Sometimes a man who has been in a long time will quit because he's done something, and he knows how hard It will be on him to get back. He either faces It or he don't. That's up to the person. But if he don't face It, he will go down. He will slowly sink down with nothing but dust in him. He will be half alive until he dies and he won't be human any more.

The Stranger and the Spider

ONE TIME A STRANGER came to one of them big Tipi Meetings. He just sat there while everybody was singing and praying. The people didn't trust him. They was suspicious that he had bad thoughts because he sat so quiet looking down.

Finally one of the Members said he saw a big spider crawl out from the Moon beside the Peyote Chief. He said he saw the spider crawl slowly around the circle and then it crawled right up the leg of the stranger and into his shirt pocket. The stranger didn't seem to notice it.

Everyone was watching and wondering what would happen. The man who seen this and told the people about it said it must be a sign the stranger had bad thoughts in his mind. They waited all morning to see what the spider would do. But nothing happened.

Finally, during open time of the Meeting, the man asked the stranger, 'Why don't you feel in your pocket and see what is there?' The stranger was very quiet, but he did what the man said. Everybody was watching him close. He reached in and felt around in his pocket. Then he pulled out a big folded silk handkerchief.

All the people was excited and ready to drive him away. They all looked at him hard and said, 'Let us see what you got in that handkerchief!'

The stranger opened his handkerchief. Inside, was a beautiful big green Peyote...the Chief kind.

Then everyone felt ashamed because now they knew what the spider was. It was the Peyote showing them something about their thoughts.

Straight with the Medicine

EVERYBODY HERE knows me. I been coming to these Meetings a long time. Seems like everybody here got something to say. I ain't said much for a long time, because I came here to learn from the people. But now I want to say something. If you are too quiet the people start to wonder about you. I want the people here to know what I'm thinking. If I got anything bad on my mind, I want the people to hear it. If I got good in my mind, I want these people to hear it.

I been trying to do some good for myself here and I been trying to do my part to help. When I say I been coming along this Way a long time, I don't mean that is so much. I'm still the same dumb Indian just doing his best to get along. There are plenty of smart guys around here. Well, that's all right. But I been trying a little all the time. I been coming here because I got no place else to go. I keep coming because what I'm trying to get to is right here in this Tipi, right here in this Medicine, and right here with the people. I know maybe I can find something here. I never felt that no place else.

One thing I learned about this Church we got here is that you got to tell the truth. If you got the Medicine in you, you got to do it or you feel worse. The Medicine makes it that way. If you said some thing bad against someone it's best to tell them and get it out. Then the Medicine treats you right. I seen that work. My friend over there can tell you. One time he didn't tell me something he had on his mind about me. It made him sick all night at the Meeting. Then my other friend there tells him to come and tell me in the morning. He did, and he felt better right away.

There was that guy we all know down in the valley. One time he said something real bad against our friend here .He didn't feel too good until he came and told it to everybody at a Meeting. I heard that, and I saw both of them guys real happy talking the next morning. Another time, that same guy come to a Meeting not feeling too good. He told everybody he was sick because when he was skinning a deer it kicked him in the chest. The people started to pray for him. But the Roadchief knew he wasn't telling the truth. He spoke right out and said this guy was having trouble with his wife and that's what hurt him in the chest. But that guy didn't want to admit it. If he only said the truth at that Meeting it would really help him. But he lied that time.

That's the way the Medicine is, and that's something I learned here.

Some people around here got some ideas in their mind about me. Maybe they don't like some of my ways too much. But they ain't said anything right out to me. Last night when I was singing, one guy here I think is my friend was holding up his fan at me like maybe I was Coyote or something. Maybe he was trying to do something to me. I don't know. But he ain't said nothing to me. You don't do that to a friend. Maybe he will say something to me today.

Some people don't seem to want me to help. I learned you can't be straight with this Medicine unless you do your part. This Roadchief we got here now seems to have pretty good thoughts, I think. He seems to be serious in the way he leads us along. But I been coming here every time and no one asks me to be Cedar Chief or Drum Chief yet. I want to help, but it seems like they don't think I'm ready for it yet. Well, I know I got a long way to go, but my friends should tell me why they don't want me to help that way.

I try to keep that out of my mind. I think maybe my friends are waiting to see what kind of man I am. But they been waiting a long time and maybe they see something they don't like. Well, they got to tell the truth sometime. And I been trying to help anyway. For a long time I been the one who makes the outfits for some of the leaders here. I don't ask for no pay for that. I figure it will make our Church fine here, and it's something I know how to do.

I made some real pretty fans and staffs with real fancy beadwork and special feathers I saved for a long time. I made some rattles it took me a long time to finish. You got to keep them gourds a long time and rub them until they get thin and hard like shells. That way, when you put them on the handle with a piece of abalone shell at the bottom and seven little Stars of quartz rock inside, they sound high and clear like ice breaking. Some people I know over in California say my stuff looks better than what them Indians down in Arizona or way back East been making. I don't know about that. But the people here I been making these outfits for never said anything like that to me. Maybe they don't think it is too good. But they use them anyway. I see some right here.

Back there a couple months ago the people were talking about how we was getting low on the Medicine. They said maybe we ought to send somebody down to Texas to get some more. But nobody did nothing about it. Then I said I would try to make the run down to the Gardens. Two of my friends here said they would help too. We started taking up some donations from the Members. Some of the ladies here went around asking people to help, and they make cake and coffee to encourage the people. At one Meeting we had some money piled up in the middle. Even some of our friends from down in the valley put in a little, though they was just visiting our Meeting.

But then it seemed like somebody didn't want us to go. One of the Members here looked like he had something on his mind. He said, 'It seems like some of our Members is getting hungry.' Now that wasn't right to say and it was no joke. But we went anyway. We had only that little money from the donations and we used most of our own cash for the trip.

We made that trip in a few days. Nobody got tired. We didn't sleep once. Nobody got hungry. We didn't have no flat tires and that old car kept moving as long as we was singing. We kept passing through towns and moving over the road like the wheels wasn't on the ground. We didn't make dust. We saw people looking at us going by like we was something they never seen before.

We made it. We found where the Medicine grows. We was singing there and had a couple little Meetings there. We prayed all the time on that trip. We prayed to the Medicine where It was growing in that grey sand like they got in Texas. We made it back the same way…like we ain't been gone but one night. We had plenty of Medicine…a big bag of fine green buttons with tufts like Chiefs. We was kept going by taking plenty of that green fresh Medicine. It is something nobody can forget about.

But when we got back and started giving out the Medicine, that same Member says to me, 'It shouldn't take any more money to take that trip than to stay home.' I felt bad about the way he said that. But I just said, 'It's easier to stay home and talk than to help the people get their Medicine.'

Now I don't mind too much about that, because I was lucky to have the chance to go down there and see the Gardens where the Medicine grows. Us few guys will never forget that trip, and when we go again we will know what to do. But nobody here asked us to tell about that time. Nobody thanked us or prayed for us for doing that.

That's something I been thinking about. I'm no stranger here. I'm some kind of person. But I don't hear nobody pray for me. I come here to learn and to hear good things and maybe do myself some good. I always pray for the other people, but it seems like when the praying is going around they pass me by. Sometimes I come to these Meetings looking for some kind of help. Sometimes I don't feel too strong inside. I always think of that when I'm praying for somebody else. I'm thinking maybe that man or that lady there needs some kind of good word right now. Maybe the Medicine is waiting to hear some good word from the people to go to work for that Member. Maybe the Medicine is waiting for that good word to help me, too. So I don't worry too much, because I feel good when I pray for somebody.

But I always heard this is the place people come to help each other go straight on the Road. So I wonder who is praying for me to go straight. Maybe I don't talk out, I think. Maybe nobody knows I need help somtimes. So now I am taking my time to tell my friends here. I feel good here now. I feel strong inside and I can talk easy to my friends here.

Maybe some of the people here thinking some things about me. Maybe they heard something. People talk sometimes. Even my friends talk sometimes. I didn't start out too good in life. My family didn't like me too much. They seemed to think something was wrong with me in some kind of way. They never treated me right. Maybe they was right. When I was about eighteen I decided to go away to some other tribe where the people didn't know me and would treat me better. Some people say I was run out of the valley, but that ain't so. I went down to Mono. I stayed there a couple years. Them people was all right. I never had no trouble there.

But my family had plenty of trouble. I hardly got any family left. I had a lot of brothers. But each of them and my folks had something happen to them...got sick and died off. Some people around here know about that. There was somebody down there in the valley was responsible for that. They had some kind of way to do that. I'm the only one left of that family around here now. Them that didn't die off went away. But I want to tell you something. If it wasn't that I joined this Church and went with the Medicine I wouldn't be here myself.

People talk a lot. But I can talk too. I can talk right here and tell you why I'm not afraid of what anybody says about me. Maybe somebody here got something in their mind about what happened to my family and what people say about me. Well, here I am in person and they can tell me here in this good place.

I heard things some people been saying. Last year when that lady over there got hurt bad in a thunder storm I heard some people was saying I had something to do with it. I don't think that lady ever said that, but some people went around saying it. Why should I do something like that? I'm in this here Church now. I'm trying to be straight with the Medicine. I don't try to play around with any of them other things.

When I was a little boy down in the valley I used to go out in the fields there sometimes when it was storming. I used to like to hear the thunder and lightning. The sound of thunder seemed to hit against the mountains and bounce off and then go rolling north. While that thunder was rolling away I could hear him singing a song in that voice just like the echo thunder makes in the mountains. I remembered that song and I could sing it. It went *Li wa, liwa na.* That *li* sound is kind of white man language sound...kind of hard and rolling along...*li wan.*

I used to sing that song when I was a little boy. My family people laughed at me and tried to shame me so I would stop. They said maybe I was trying to be some kind of doctor like my old uncle who had some kind of Eagle and Lightning medicine. I didn't know about that. I just knew how to sing that song. It was my song. But it seemed like my family didn't like my ways. It seemed like they wanted to make it hard on me and I was always getting into trouble.

That's why I ran away to live with the Mono people down there. When I came back I was a grown man and I stayed away from people who didn't treat me right. Most of my family was gone by then. That's when I first started going to these meetings. That's the first time I heard of the Peyote. I had plenty troubles on my mind. I didn't feel good for nothing. My life didn't seem good to me. I couldn't seem to get along with nobody.

I heard about Sam Dick holding Meetings down there. He didn't have no Tipi then...just put up some kind of blankets to hold out the wind. But plenty people came. I never heard nothing like it. I never heard songs like that. It opened up a new life for me. The people there talked to me. They was friendly. They didn't ask me questions about who I was. They took me as a person. I went to all the Meetings I could and I hung around them people. You know, I couldn't listen to the radio no more. Because the music sounded like tin cans rattling. I didn't want to hear nothing but Indian music after that.

I was around there when it all started. That was back in the thirties, back a long time ago, and some people here never was around then. They was doing something else. Lone Bear was the first one. He came around here talking about the new Medicine. He lived with Sam Dick and he told old Sam this was a new Way of curing people and doing good. I didn't go to those old Meetings, but Sam Dick told me. Lone Bear gave him a drum one time and said, 'Just beat on it...just keep beating on it and singing…maybe somebody will hear it…somebody far away…maybe they will hear it back there where the Medicine come from…maybe it will show you a new Way…maybe somebody will come.'

About seven years after that Ben Lancaster come to Carson Valley. Then Sam Dick knew what Lone Bear said was true. Lancaster told us how to run the Meetings. He really got it started. He did it a little different than we do it now, but he was the first real Roadchief around here. Lone Bear got into trouble. He didn't stick with it.

Some of the people here don't know about all this. They wasn't in from the beginning. I know some of the people here don't think much of Ben Lancaster and Sam Dick. Well, I know they did some things different and some people didn't like it. But I got started way back then, and those old timers helped me some.

Sam Dick used to pray good. It was just like he knew everything in the world. He talked about the whole world, and he made it seem all right there in the Tipi…like the Medicine put him in contact with everything. Anyway, it seemed that way to me. Ben Lancaster, too. When he prayed, it was just like you could hear his heart beating all over the Tipi…like you could feel his blood running in his veins. That sounds funny, but sometimes it's like that. My friend over there can pray like that. Last Meeting he prayed in his own language…Shoshoni. But it was like everybody could understand what he was saying. It seemed like he was talking about them Peyote Gardens where the Medicine grows… that valley and them pretty green hills where you gather it. It was just like you could see it right there before you. It makes you feel good, like all them old Indians back there are with you.

But Sam and Ben didn't help all the time. They didn't pray for everybody…just those they wanted to pray for. They didn't let everybody in their Meetings like we do here. They told some people to stay out. One time my mother was real sick. So I asked Sam to hold a Meeting for her. But he wouldn't do it. This made me wonder about the way they were doing things down there.

That is when I heard about the new kind of Meetings they was holding up here. Sam said to me kind of mad, 'Well, I hear them guys are holding some kind of Meetings up there in the mountains...maybe you should go there...maybe they can do something for you.'

Well, I heard about this new Roadchief holding Meetings up here. I heard about how he been to Idaho and learned the real Way...the new Tipi Way. I came up here and saw him. He said he would hold a Meeting for my mother right off. We had a Meeting. She got better. I never forgot that, and that man who was the new Chief then is still my friend today. Since that time I been coming to these Meetings here. I been sticking it out with all the new things that have been coming along since that time. We got a lot of new Chiefs now, and things are coming along pretty good. I like these Meetings here, because the people are trying to help each other.

But I don't hold nothing against Sam Dick. He got me started. The Medicine helped him pretty strong. He knew just when the war was going to start in 1941. I was at the Meeting when he said he seen a bunch of big ships up in the air...like they was coming west towards America. But then he says they turned around and went back. Just a few days later, the war started. He even told me the day I would be drafted. He saw me with a uniform on. I was drafted on the day he said.

When I first came to these new Meetings up here, that Roadchief had a dream about the war too. In one of the first Meetings I come to up here he seen a little airplane fly right into the Tipi. It flew across and hit him on the forehead. Then he saw it spin down toward the Moon. The Moon became just like a sandy beach along the water. The plane crashed down right there in front of him. Just a couple weeks later the people heard about that young Washoe boy being killed in a plane crash.

The Medicine can do plenty for you. When I went in the war my friends gave me a fine big Chief button to keep on me all the time. Sometimes they sent me a little dried Medicine to keep me up. Well, I was all over that war in France and Germany and Africa. I saw people dead all around me like the end of the world. But I came through and never even got hurt. I was never even scared except one time. That time

I had to jump and hide in a ditch by the side of the road when the planes was shooting at us. While I was down there a bunch of tanks started coming by the road. They sounded like the loudest thunder I ever heard. The whole world was shaking and I thought I was finished. But I got my Chief in my hand and started singing my song loud as I could. As soon as I did that I wasn't scared no more. Everything got kind of quiet, and the tanks kept on going by like they was running on soft sand with no motors.

That's how I started to learn how strong this Medicine is if you are the right kind of person. You got to make yourself straight before It will back you up. They say It is just like electricity. It can run through you and make everything run good. You can send telegrams with It to somebody far away. But they told me the Medicine ain't to play with...not just to make people scared or surprised. It is for the health and happiness of all Indian people. It is to give them good life. You got to keep your mind on living a good life and helping other people. They say this Tipi is no doctor's house...it is a Church.

So I been trying to live straight and follow the Medicine. I don't say I've gone very far. I just keep trying. Maybe when I'm an old man I will know something But some people don't seem to respect a man for trying. It's like some people don't want another person to make it. Sometimes I don't come to Meetings for a while because of that. It makes me feel no good like I'm not worth nothing. But then my good friend over there tells me I got to stick with it. He says there will be a certain time when everything will be all right again. So I believe him.

My friend has gone on this Road a longer way than me. I started pretty bad, I guess. I got plenty work to do. My ideas ain't too straight yet. A couple weeks ago I had a dream in the Meeting that time. I saw four fine big Peyote...four Chiefs. Each one was in its own box in that grey sand like in Texas. The Chiefs come from different directions into the Tipi. They just come in floating through the air and then lined up in a row East and West. It was like they was sitting there waiting for the people to do something...maybe take sides about them or something.

I told my friend about this. I said maybe those fine big live Peyote

48

Chiefs was trying to show me how the people in these Meetings here ain't satisfied with the way their leaders is acting. Maybe it shows that different people are trying to be Roadchiefs and don't come right out and say what they is thinking. Maybe it means we got to make a choice.

This is what I asked my friend. But he said I had to get my mind straight on that. He said there is no taking sides in Peyote. All of them is good. The Peyote was telling me that all Its ways is good and you don't have to choose one. It was telling me that each man who is honest with the Medicine has his own Chief, and each Chief is as good as the other. That's why they was all in one line there...lined up. Each man's Chief is equal and good, but each man is different and one man might be far along the Road and another man not so far. So that's something I learned from my friend. Now I got them ideas out of my mind about people here not agreeing.

Some people here got things on their mind they don't tell me. Maybe they think I'm trying to use some different ways because of what they heard somewhere. They know me a long time yet they might think that about me. I heard that's not the way the real Medicine tells us to think. You don't hold bad thoughts about other Members. You got to say it out plain to him so he can answer.

When I was a young guy I had some kind of idea in me like that, I guess. I liked to hear thunder and had a special song. I didn't know what it meant but it seemed to cause me some trouble. Then I got scared of it. When I started to come to Meetings I didn't like to hear thunder no more. But I kept singing my song. When I was singing that song I didn't think nothing could hurt me.

One time I was in a Meeting. I was using my song when the drum come around to me. One guy I knew then who acted like he was my friend was drumming for me. We didn't have a Tipi then...only blankets hung up for the wind. The sky was dark and clear...no clouds and you could see all the stars. I was singing and looking up at the sky with my eyes sort of closed. But there was something funny about the drum. It didn't sound right. It sounded like a kind of rumble like thunder...or like a big generator running in the sky. Then some drops of water splashed on my face and arms. It was like rain, but the sky was clear. I looked at this guy who was drumming for me. He was smiling at me like he knew what was happening. I didn't understand it. I didn't feel good about him. I thought maybe it was the drum splashing water on me, but I wasn't wet. I was scared, so I kept my song going strong. It didn't happen again, so I felt all right. No one else at the Meeting knew about that. But I think about it often.

After the Meeting this guy who drummed for me said why don't I stay at his place down in Antelope Valley that night. We got there when it was just dark. It was a small old place out by itself near the salt flat. When we was there talking for a while he said he had to go in town to get something. He said for me to go ahead and get some sleep. I was sleeping for a long time when something made me wake up. I could hear something walking around out in the sagebrush. I looked out the window but couldn't see nothing. Pretty soon it was running around the cabin close by. I yelled out my friend's name, but he didn't answer.

Just then I heard something coming up on the porch. It was scratching on the door. I think maybe it is my friend, so I opened the door. In front of my face was a big Coyote head with its hair stuck out stiff and eyes like pieces of burning charcoal. I banged the door shut right on that face. I was so scared I couldn't breath. I started to sing my song as loud as I could. I put my mind on the Medicine and kept praying for It to help me. Pretty soon I heard steps going away. A little while later I heard some Coyotes barking and one loud one howling. I couldn't sleep the rest of the night...just sat in that cabin taking Medicine and singing.

Next morning, about light, this guy who owns the place come back. He said his car broke down and he had to stay in town all night. He asks if I'm okay. I say, 'Yes I'm OK.' But I don't tell him nothing about that night. He kept looking around the place like he lost something. He went outside and looked all over the porch and the ground. Then I saw him pick up something out in the sagebrush. He put it in his pocket and came back. He said, 'Well, now you know where my place is...you can come stay anytime.'

He wanted to take me home in his car. I said, 'No, I like to walk.' I never went back there, and when that guy was at Meetings I never sat near him again. I ain't seen him for a long time.

I didn't try to get any ideas from that. I tried to keep my mind straight on the Medicine and not think bad of that guy. That is what the Medicine shows you. I pray for him when I get the chance. I think maybe he is in real trouble. He was keeping something from me. If he was straight with the Medicine he wouldn't do that. He would come and tell me what it was. But he never has done that.

Another time, much later, when I started coming to these Meetings here, I was praying hard one night because I had lots of things bothering me. It was in the Tipi but when I looked up I saw the sky...real blue and deep like I was looking into empty space. Then I felt something was coming down from over my shoulder, coming down from way up in the sky. I looked up and there was a big cross like the one Jesus was crucified on. It was the biggest one I ever saw...as big as a building...not like them little ones people wear around their neck. It was coming down on two big chains out of the sky. I couldn't see where the chains come from. Then, just as it was coming down, there was a flash of lightning and loud thunder. The lightning flashed white right across the sky and cut those big chains right off. That cross started to fall slowly and to tip over towards me. It was falling slowly right on me.

I got scared and opened my eyes. I had to shake that off. I came back right there in the Tipi, and all the people was there just the same, and one Member was singing good. I don't know what that dream means. Maybe it means that kind ain't for me. Maybe it was some kind of warning. The lightning was the white kind...not the blue flash kind I usually see.

But that same Meeting I saw something else. After Midnight one man there was singing fine. I asked the Chief for smoke and prayed for the people who was sick there. I prayed for myself, too. I prayed to learn the real truth, so my mind would get clear. I prayed to the Medicine to help poor dumb Indians like me. I prayed to feel strong and good. Well, then, just when I finished, I was looking into the fire and saw a beautiful fan with spotted white and brown feathers like eagle or hawk. It was real pretty, just like looking at feathers in front of light. The feathers was all spread out even and flat…just right. It was like there was bright shining daylight on the other side of the fan. I could see right through it. On the other side was a real good looking man with sort of light skin. He was standing straight with real Indian headgear on…all fine feathers. He had a sort of thin face…a real fine looking man…sort of proud and serious.

He was singing a beautiful song. It was like the song a Member was singing in the Meeting. It was just like that man was singing. But it was like my song, too. When I looked at the feathers on the man's head, I saw blue light coming up from his head like lightning stretching out… spreading out like a fan so bright it hurt my eyes. But there was no thunder. I don't know if that was real or just in my mind. But it was strong, and I felt it was the real thing the Medicine was showing me. I felt like I was getting on the other side for just a second and seeing what the Medicine had to tell me.

I talked to my real friends about that. They told me not to worry. They said I am coming along…learning just a little. They said maybe what I see at the Meetings tells me my song is okay as long as I use it for the good of myself and the people. They said maybe the Peyote is trying to show me the people should not be afraid of old Indian ways as long as they use them right. Maybe the Medicine changes all that and turns it into good. Everything depends on keeping straight with the Medicine.

List of Illustrations

Waterbird (title page): A traditional symbol of the sacred bird of waters common to many North American Indian cultures, and in the Peyote religion.

Peyote (page one): The Peyote cactus, *Lophophora williamsii*, which is the sacrament of the Peyote religion. It is a small, spineless, tufted plant which grows in semi-desert regions from Texas and New Mexico, in the north, to south-central Mexico.

Tipi (page three): The traditional meeting place of the Peyote congregation, the Tipi Way.

Star (page eight): A traditional symbol denoting the stars of the sky and the seven-pointed design created on the bottom of the iron kettle drum when the deerskin is properly stretched and tied with thongs.

Rattle (page fourteen): The beaded and hafted gourd rattle used to accompany Peyote songs.

Sunburst (page nineteen): Printer's design.

Fan (page twenty-two): The feather fan which has profound significance in Peyote ceremonials.

Fire (page twenty-seven): The sacred fire of the Peyote ceremony.

Moon (page twenty-nine): The crescent-shaped earthen altar of the Peyote Meeting, grooved by a line suggesting the Peyote Road and centered by a Chief Peyote. The Ash Moon is a smaller crescent formed by raking together the accumulating embers of the fire.

Man on a Donkey (page thirty-two): Adapted from an Apache basket in the Denver Art Museum.

Peyote Chief (page thirty-four): The large dried crown of the Peyote plant which is kept as a special emblem and guide by a Peyotist leader.

Church (page thirty-six): Adapted from a Mission Indian basket.

Spider (page thirty-nine): A major element in the narrative.

Waterbird (page forty): A traditional symbol among American Indian people and of the Peyote Way. (See also title page.)

Warren L. d'Azevedo is professor of Anthropology at the University of Nevada, Reno. A graduate of the University of California, Berkeley, and recipient of the doctorate from Northwestern University in 1962, his research includes extensive periods of field study in West Africa and among the Washoe people of California and Nevada. He is contributor to and editor of the "Great Basin" volume of the new *Handbook of North American Indians* published by the Smithsonian Institution.